KAVANAGH COUNTRY

KAVANAGH COUNTRY

EDITED BY PJ BROWNE

PHOTOGRAPHS BY DAVID MAHER

First published in 2009 by

CURRACH PRESS

55A Spruce Avenue, Stillorgan Industrial Park, Blackrock, County Dublin

www.currach.ie

1 3 5 4 2

Design by bluett

Cover photographs by David Maher

Printed by ColourBooks, Baldoyle Industrial Estate, Dublin 13

ISBN: 978-1-85607-969-3

Contents

PREFACE

John B. Keane sparked my early interest in Kavanagh. I have the (borrowed) notes from a lecture he gave in UCC in November 1974. I met 'Johneen' again during a teaching stint he did at Seton Hall University, New Jersey. The Theatre in the Round (Celtic Theatre) introduced his plays to countless Americans and Irish-Americans.

I got to know Peter Kavanagh in the mid-1990s. Our initial chats dealt with a proposed article for *Irish Runner* magazine. Frank Greally, founder and editor of the magazine, was aware of the young Patrick Kavanagh's athletic abilities but wasn't convinced that the poet had been talented enough to run a sub-five-minute mile. Peter Kavanagh put the record straight on that in short order. This was a trivial enough matter but he insisted on accuracy. There is a perception that Peter was arrogant like his brother Patrick – but without the genius. On the contrary, I found him very enthusiastic and generous with his time. When I told him my father was a shoemaker (not the pejorative 'cobbler'), who had been apprenticed for two years in Dublin, he became animated and genuinely interested. I must have passed his test because he never failed to return a call or answer a query.

Dáithí Ó hÓgáin, as always, was an inspiration and generous with his support.

A special thank-you to the Library of Congress, Washington DC. I could not have negotiated this labyrinthine facility without the advice of Audrey Teague of the American Library Association.

Daragh O'Malley, actor and son of Hilda and Donogh O'Malley, Bruce Arnold, Con Houlihan and the late Dr Patrick Hillery provided valuable information. Thanks to Frank Greally for many kindnesses.

David Maher took all the beautiful pictures that appear in the book. I greatly value our friendship, which goes back many years. When David was taking photographs in and around Inniskeen, the following people were very helpful to him: Rosaleen Kearney and Briege Byrne of the Patrick Kavanagh Centre; Nuala Devlin (McNello's Pub); Alan O'Rourke (Inniskeen Station); Tom Rooney (Billy Brennan's Barn); and Thomas Dooley (Kednaminsha School).

My thanks also to Jo O'Donoghue and Currach Press, to Syd Bluett, who designed the cover and interior of this book, to Jonathan Williams of the Jonathan Williams Literary Agency, to the Trustees of the Estate of the late Katherine B. Kavanagh and to Antoinette Quinn, Kavanagh's editor and biographer, for textual elucidation.

Finally, I wish to acknowledge the unwavering support of Susan, Patrick and Claire Browne.

PJ Browne
New York, October 2009

Patrick Kavanagh (1904–67)

Patrick Kavanagh was born on Sunday 21 October 1904. He was the fourth child (and first son) born to James and Bridget Kavanagh in the townland of Mucker, Inniskeen parish, County Monaghan. This is not to be confused with the village of Inniskeen, less than a mile from the Kavanaghs' home but outside the childhood landscape of the poet.

Kavanagh's family home was located on the Mucker lane, a stone's-throw off the main Inniskeen to Carrickmacross road. The Carrickmacross to Dundalk railway line ran parallel to the main road with its crossing gates and gatehouse.

It was a small community of about thirty families living within a radius of less than a mile. Poverty and the struggle to eke out a living were common to all the houses. The crumbling vestiges of the Kenny estate and its big house were a reminder of the former Ascendancy rule.

Kavanagh's earliest memories wandered back to the Mucker lane on the north side of the house which led up to the main Inniskeen road. The lane took him past Cassidy's, Lennon's, Cullen's. On the south side of the house were the dunghill, the sheds and a yard, the focus of the family's farming lives. The surrounding fields were predominantly bog: streams, ditches, banks and weeds dominated this heavy, unyielding soil. The higher ground was more amenable to fitful cultivation.

The homestead was originally a thatched house. Kavanagh's father turned it into a two-storey dwelling with a slate roof in 1909. A year later he bought land across the bog and divided it into three fields. Three cows were purchased, which gave the family the status of small farmers.

When he was four years old Patrick went to school at nearby Kednaminsha, where he was taught 'the three Rs' by a strict Miss Cassidy. On leaving school he was apprenticed to his father, who was a qualified shoemaker. Patrick paid little or no attention to the trade, much to the consternation of the family. Even at the best of times, shoemaking of the traditional kind brought in an erratic and unreliable income. The making and repairing of shoes was a slow process and financial remuneration might come much later.

As Ireland grappled with its new-found independence and Civil War, there was scarcely any interest in politics in the Kavanagh household. W.B. Yeats's articulation of the idea of a distinctive national literature would have been unknown in Kavanagh's country. However, it was from this impoverished area that one of the most articulate challengers to that romantic vision would emerge.

The family decided to buy a small farm called Reynolds's Farm, a half-mile from the house. It consisted of seven small fields, waterlogged, with heavy clay. However, it had the potential to be productive with ploughing and drainage. With that in mind, they purchased an old mare and a second-hand cart. The major family decisions were taken by Bridget Kavanagh, a shrewd woman when it came to the handling of important household matters and, of course, money.

Kavanagh began to write juvenile verse sometime after his twelfth birthday. There is no explanation as to why he began to write verse. An explanation is hardly necessary anyway. As the poet reflected, he began to dabble in verse and then discovered it was his life. Far from being viewed as a harmless pastime by his family, it was regarded as a waste of time. In their eyes he could have put his time to better use; there was plenty of work around the farm.

A more negative attitude surfaced when the family could not dissuade him from this activity. Their biggest fear was that he would not only embarrass the family but bring scandal on them. According to his brother Peter: 'Poetry was viewed as something feckless, even dangerous. To be considered a bard in the locality was very unsettling. Patrick was regarded as a bit of a "gom" a class of an idiot for pursuing this. The family took it very bad and they were not slow in telling him. My sisters were quite hard on him and some of the criticism was hurtful.'[1]

The family's attitude was to be expected and when the father died in 1929, Patrick's position became more marginalised. The man of the family, aged twenty-five, the hope for the future of the farm, was squandering his time reading literature and writing verse. In September 1928 his poem 'Freedom' was placed second in a competition run by the *Irish Weekly Independent*. Within a year he had published fourteen poems in the newspaper.

This might have signalled his arrival as a poet but it enhanced his feeling of estrangement and otherness, which was to remain with him until he died. He made his first pilgrimage to Dublin to see Æ; his desire to venture away from the farm was growing and he was anxious to see what might be in store for him in Dublin. He made several visits to the capital over the next seven years, fitting these trips around his duties on the farm.

His literary contacts grew more numerous and his reputation was burnished by the publication of *Ploughman and Other Poems* (1936). He struggled with the decision to leave the security and familiarity of the farm behind him. It was a predictable and in many ways a pleasant life but the oppression he felt and the notion of living among people who openly derided his creativity was frustrating. His days on the farm in Inniskeen were numbered.

Kavanagh was a tall rangy individual; he was also a restless sort. He liked to test himself by jumping over ditches;

running also appealed to him. He was fit enough to run a mile in under five minutes and maintained a lifelong interest in athletics. The physical side of life on the farm filled his days and the rest of his time was devoted to reading and writing. He was a non-drinker; alcohol did not become a presence until he moved to Dublin.

Whatever aspirations Kavanagh had for inclusion in Dublin literary circles were quickly tempered. He did little to help his cause. He came across as a hard person to like, even when sober. The publication of *Ploughman* fixed his image as the peasant poet.

THE DECLINE OF SIMPLICITY

Kavanagh moved to Dublin in 1939 on a more or less permanent basis. He had ventured to London in 1937, with high hopes based on correspondence with literary contacts. *The Green Fool* was published a year later (1938) and, despite his later misgivings about it, the book embedded the image of Kavanagh as a writer with peasant qualities.

There was a patronising connotation to the 'peasant poet' image. His Dublin detractors regarded him as a poet of marginal significance. Kavanagh's searing realism ran counter to the romantic depictions made fashionable by the literary revival. The Inniskeen man was the genuine article. There is a sense in which he was too real for a lot of people. He did not change no matter what the context; he was one of those who changed least with external pressure. A writer is often outside his society. Kavanagh was both outside and inside.

He had a keen realisation of his own nature, a nature utterly unpretentious. His ambivalence about his move to Dublin was never resolved. The shrewd small-farmer mentality would cause him to question the wisdom of the decision.

It was the worst mistake of my life. The Hitler war had started. I had my comfortable little holding of watery hills beside the Border. What was to bate it for a life? And yet I wasted what could have been my four glorious years, begging and scrambling around the streets of malignant Dublin.[2]

There is more than a hint of bitterness in this reflection. By his own admission, Kavanagh was not a literary success in Dublin. He was never going to be popular with the literary establishment in the city. He was quick to air his frustration, anger and disappointment in his columns and essays. His negative appraisal of the literary scene deepened the bias against him.

Between 1939 and 1955, Kavanagh produced his finest writing, including, as well as poetry, several dozen essays, human-interest stories, articles and innumerable book reviews. He developed his own distinctive point of view that, as he once said, seemed to be everything.

Kavanagh seemed to enjoy his reputation as a difficult, cantankerous character, assuming overbearing poses in pub conversations and in his newspaper pieces. He was surly and contentious but above all else he was poor. His work as a writer never paid well. Without the support of his brother Peter, it would have been impossible for him to continue living in Dublin. Peter's job as a teacher ensured that he had a place to stay and enough to eat but little else.

This essentially hand-to-mouth existence impinged on his poetry, which became increasingly satirical, at times savagely so. His journalism allowed him to berate the urbane and patronising civil servants, office clerks and the pseudo-artistic, who congregated in the Palace Bar. His summary dismissal of Dubliners and their lack of talent inevitably made enemies. By way of getting back at the poet innumerable stories were told about his boorish behaviour, some true, others embellished or made up. They became part of Dublin's social currency.

'He had,' wrote Anthony Cronin, 'good reason for adopting some of the attitudes that he did to the scene around him and for regarding the much more comfortable dispositions that others seemed able to make of their very much lesser talents and their lives with envy and even rage.'[3] If Kavanagh had a grievance and sense of entitlement, it surely derived from the struggle to make ends meet.

He wrote sporadically for *The Irish Times*, the *Standard* and the *Irish Independent*. The *Irish Press* hired him, beginning on 14 September 1942, to write a twice-weekly column entitled 'City Commentary.' Using the pseudonym 'Piers Plowman', Kavanagh's intention was to portray a countryman's impression of city life for the benefit of his rural friends. For the next eighteen months he attended race meetings, parades, football matches and numerous social events.

In 1943 the *Standard* hired him to write a weekly column called 'Literary Scene'. Although this was ostensibly a book review, Kavanagh wrote more often about literary happenings in Dublin. The temptation to express his own point of view proved too great. Two essays, 'The Road to Nowhere' and 'The Anglo-Irish Mind' hastened his exit from the *Standard* and Benedict Kiely replaced him after four months.

Kavanagh's defining work, *The Great Hunger*, was written in October 1941. His brother Peter remembered:

> He showed me the first pages of it when I came home from school one afternoon and I knew that he was closing in, as it were, on something very special. He asked my opinion of it, as he had done since he first began to write verse. I encouraged him to stay at it and he did. He was at the height of his physical and mental powers, a mere thirty-seven years old. He had fierce energy during those years. He finished the poem in eighteen days.[4]

The poem was published as an expensive edition by the Yeats sisters' Cuala Press in 1942, so was read at the time by only a handful of people. *Lough Derg*, Kavanagh's last long poem, was written in the summer of 1942 and was posthumously printed. Macmillan collected the poetry of the war years in *A Soul For Sale* (1947). This volume and *The Great Hunger* reached a wider audience.

It was this epic poem that first drew John B. Keane to Kavanagh. He befriended Kavanagh and drank with him in McDaid's and Neary's. They enjoyed each other's company and later appeared on a weekly television show, *Pick of the Post*, along with the actor Joe Lynch and model Betty Whelan. Joe Linnane presented the programme.

Keane remembered the furore when *The Great Hunger* was published:

> The opening section of the poem was first published in the Irish number of *Horizon* (January 1942) and after it appeared in the bookshops the authorities seized it on the grounds of indecency. I don't know that it was actually banned but we'll say it was semi-banned. I remember well the day my father flung a copy of the poem on the table exclaiming, 'There's a great poem for you.'[5]

Kavanagh believed that his future as a writer was in England – there was more work, a wider audience and the remuneration was better. The Second World War essentially closed off this option to him. In February 1946, Kavanagh was back with the *Standard* as a film critic. His weekly 'Round the Cinemas' ran for a little over three years. His reviews were negative and caustic and it didn't take long for boredom to set in. He lost patience with the contrived plots and dialogue and his disdain for film as an artistic medium was very obvious.

He broadened the scope of the column to include literary and social criticism and railed at the bogus image of Ireland portrayed in newspapers and magazines. With the exception of Samuel Beckett, James Joyce, W.H. Auden and a few others, Kavanagh concluded that all writers were cultureless mediocrities. This critical assessment of mostly Irish art and culture continued when he was given a monthly 'Diary' at *Envoy*.

In April 1952, Kavanagh, with the financial backing of his brother Peter, began writing and publishing *Kavanagh's Weekly*. Although it ran for a mere thirteen weeks, it gave Kavanagh a platform to examine Irish society. It was blunt and controversial but above all refreshing. All aspects of Irish life were scrutinised. The journal was witty and lively but antagonised many. Lack of financial support and poor distribution were the main reasons for its demise.

Kavanagh was disappointed and unsettled by the failure of the journal. In the ensuing two years, disappointment gave way to disillusionment as a result of the infamous libel case against the *Leinster Leader*. In October 1952, a somewhat one-sided profile of him was published in the *Leinster Leader*. Kavanagh's immediate response was to file a libel action against the newspaper's publishers. The profile was essentially innocuous and similar to what Kavanagh had been writing over the years. Poverty and the chance to make a quick financial killing prompted the poet to take this ill-judged action. His litigious small-farmer disposition was another factor and he totally misread the situation. The court case that followed was sensational.

The publishers engaged John A. Costello, in between stints as Taoiseach, as senior counsel. Costello's legendary status in legal circles was well merited. He revelled in the spotlight in his cross-examination of Kavanagh. Costello was an old-school barrister, sometimes savage, and he used every legal manoeuvre to diminish the poet. His affectation of being ignorant of literature played well with the jury. Legally it was no contest. However, Kavanagh got the better of many exchanges with Costello, who emerged as cynical and shallow – more politician than barrister.

The decision went against Kavanagh: there would be no financial bonanza. His lawyers appealed and a retrial was ordered after a lengthy argument before the Supreme Court. The newspaper could not afford any further legal action, a small settlement was arranged and the matter ended. It was a victory for the cultureless mediocrities.

Costello returned to lead the country and, in an affected gesture of remorse (and only after repeated exhortations by the poet), arranged that Kavanagh should receive an annual stipend for a series of lectures in UCD.

Defeat in the libel case had a profound effect on Kavanagh. It was a gruelling ordeal for the poet; he collapsed in court on the sixth day of the trial after thirteen hours of unrelenting cross-examination. He was too ill to attend the verdict and rested in the nearby Four Courts Hotel. He had been drinking heavily and his health was in general decline. Kavanagh viewed himself as a victim, punished by a society

he had hoped to enlighten.

Archbishop McQuaid was kind to Kavanagh and offered to pay his medical expenses. This was certainly an incongruous association – the prince of the Irish Church coming to the aid of the man who had written about masturbation in *The Great Hunger* a few years before. When he was on the touch, the poet would sometimes head to Drumcondra, although it bothered him to be treated no better than a beggar and made to wait until McQuaid saw fit to see him.

Kavanagh was never completely at a loss when he needed money. The women in his life were quite willing to assist him and there was some money coming from the farm in Inniskeen. Hilda O'Malley (née Moriarty), wife of Fianna Fáil politician Donogh O'Malley, the so-called great love of his life, kept in touch with him as she reared her family in Limerick. Notwithstanding the sentiments in 'On Raglan Road,' they were not lovers but the west Kerry woman was concerned for his welfare. She often reminded her husband Donogh to 'see if you can get something done about Kavanagh'. Being a doctor she was well aware that Kavanagh's drinking and smoking and his loss of a lung to cancer had compromised his health.

Donogh O'Malley and Patrick Kavanagh died within months of each other. O'Malley, acting on Hilda's instructions, sent a wreath of roses to Kavanagh's funeral in the shape of the letter 'H'.

Anthony Cronin, who had known Kavanagh since 1951, was a kind and compassionate figure in Kavanagh's life until his death in 1967. Cronin, perhaps more than others, witnessed the ravages caused by Kavanaghs's alcoholism.

In 1955 it was discovered that Kavanagh had cancer of the lung and required immediate surgery. He entered the Rialto Hospital in March and the diseased lung was removed. There was a widespread belief that he would not survive and his condition was very serious for several days. Even Kavanagh feared the worst and had a will drawn up before he entered the hospital. *The Irish Times* prepared an obituary about him. Against heavy odds he survived and, as he often remarked, disappointed many people.

He spent most of that summer in Dublin and it was during the warm months of July and August that his so called 'rebirth' took place on the banks of the Grand Canal. Kavanagh believed that following his illness he was reborn as a poet and little he had written before that was poetry. He spoke about a mystical experience where he realised that the important thing was to put no importance on anything.

His poetry reveals a man who survived with a more humane and carefree attitude. The criticism was not as vicious; much of the old venom was tempered. Whether this new phase is a rebirth, a return to old simplicities or the evolution of a specific poetics is open to debate. What matters is the brevity of this creativity. His increasing dependence on alcohol was the primary factor.

According to Anthony Cronin's account, Kavanagh would arrive in the office of *Envoy* in Grafton Street around noon. For a couple of hours he would read the morning's post and comment on whatever contributions he got his hands on. In the afternoon they would head over to McDaid's. 'Kavanagh drank stout in those days as a staple and was seldom drunk, or at least any drunker than the rest of us,' Anthony Cronin recalled:

> The whiskey-drinking began…during what were for Kavanagh the bad years of nineteen-fifty-three and fifty-four, the years of the libel action and undiagnosed cancer. Unfortunately, he proved an addict of a ferocious order…[6]

Cronin published many of Kavanagh's poems in *The Bell*. Kavanagh's rebirth or maturing as a poet was not lost on Cronin, who regarded the verse as 'the first examples of the kind of poetry that made him important'. Most of these poems from the mid-1950s later appeared in *Come Dance with Kitty Stobling* (1960).

In the spring of 1958, Kavanagh began a weekly column for the *Irish Farmers' Journal*. This was a sustained period of writing for the poet and he covered a wide range of material. Of the more than two hundred columns he wrote, more than half were devoted to his time on the farm in Monaghan and his life in Dublin. They were sentimental and nostalgic but struck a chord with his readers. More important, they did not require a lot of time or preparation – which suited Kavanagh. The same inward look and softer attitude were in evidence here. His poetry-writing was effectively at an end. The growing influence of alcohol dulled the creative impulse.

Socially, he was engaging and amiable company, after he had consumed just the right amount of whiskey. He remained active, with visits to London and New York. He retained a belief that London was still the best place to gain the recognition and prestige that he hankered after. His weekly column with the *Farmers' Journal* ended in March 1963. He began his last serial writing for the *RTV Guide* in 1964. By this time the effects of his alcoholism were very apparent to those close to him.

Cronin witnessed Kavanagh's delusions and irrational fears when the poet stayed with him. He needed a whiskey bottle under his pillow in case he woke at night. He was frightened of the dark. His physical and psychological health was in serious decline. His desire to write poetry disappeared as his condition worsened. Indeed his ability to muster up any motivation for proposed collections of his poetry was severely challenged. At the same time, even through the haze of alcohol, he was troubled by the belief that English and American critics ignored him.

According to his brother:

> Patrick wasn't able to stop the drink for any extended period of time so he had no chance to recover. The whiskey was the finish of him. The cumulative effects of that addiction were bound to catch up to him. I don't know how he survived as long as he did. He must have had the constitution of a horse.[7]

The collection of thirty-four poems published as *Come Dance with Kitty Stobling* was a financial success, the most successful book of poetry Kavanagh had published. By November 1960 it had sold over 2000 copies and was in its third printing. His *Collected Poems* (1964) was followed by *Collected Pruse* [Prose] (1967). He wrote the text of *Self-Portrait*, a documentary for Teilifís Éireann, in September 1962 and also made a recording, *Almost Everything* (Claddagh Records 1963).

Patrick Kavanagh married Katherine Moloney in Dublin in April 1967. Katherine was a friend of the poet Leland Bardwell and Anthony Cronin's wife Thérèse: Kavanagh had met her in London in 1957.

During his final stay in Inniskeen (two days before he died) Kavanagh repeatedly told his sisters: 'I've a feeling of death on me and I want to be buried in Inniskeen.'[8]

Patrick Kavanagh died in a Dublin nursing home on 30 November 1967. He is buried in Inniskeen.

In the forty years since Kavanagh's death his legacy has been reappraised. He may not have achieved his potential; equally, given his circumstances, his achievement was considerable. Maybe he did have much to be thankful for at the end of his days. His poetry was placed on the Irish secondary school curriculum in June 1967. In October of that same year he was given a British Arts Council award. He got nothing by way of subsidy or pension from the Irish state. The reality was that he had little enough to be thankful for. What he did have, however, was acknowledged stature as Ireland's leading poet.

Seamus Heaney was among the many poets of later generations to be inspired and influenced by Kavanagh. Heaney and his generation were moved by 'something new, authentic and liberating'[9] in Kavanagh's poetry.

It is appropriate to let the poet have the final say:

> There are two kinds of simplicity, the simplicity of going away and the simplicity of return. The last is the ultimate in sophistication....
>
> Curious this, how I had started off with the right simplicity, indifferent to crude reason, and then ploughed my way through complexities and anger, hatred and ill-will towards the faults of man, and came back to where I started.[10]

Notes

1. Peter Kavanagh: interview with the author.
2. Patrick Kavanagh, *Self-Portrait*, RTÉ television, 30 October 1962.
3. Anthony Cronin, *Dead as Doornails*, p. 85.
4. Peter Kavanagh: interview with the author.
5. John B. Keane, *Limerick Leader*, 2 February 1963.
6. Anthony Cronin, *Dead as Doornails*, p. 78.
7. Peter Kavanagh: interview with the author.
8. Patrick Kavanagh, *Self-Portrait*, RTÉ television, 30 October 1962.
9. Seamus Heaney, 'From Monaghan to the Grand Canal: The Poetry of Patrick Kavanagh' in *Preoccupations: Selected Prose 1968–78*, p. 116.
10. RTÉ archives, 'Gods Make Their Own Importance', 8 April 1973.

PART I

MONAGHAN COUNTRY: 'THE SIMPLICITY OF RETURN...'

'...the simplicity of return. The last
is the ultimate in sophistication.
In the final simplicity we don't care
whether we appear foolish or not.
We talk of things that earlier would
embarrass. We are satisfied with
being ourselves, however small.'

Self-Portrait

Some Evocations of No Importance

'What were the happiest moments in your life?' a man asked me one day. The happiest moments are those that are most vivid in the imagination. The imagination is, I think, incapable of evoking moments of sorrow....

It is a summer's day and I am aged around twenty-two and I am drawing me coal from the station....

Ah, the fields looked at me more than I at them, and at this moment they are still staring at me. The humpy hill beyond the railway at the Beeog's lane....

Somebody is driving a sow up the hill. I don't suppose I was ever up in that field. And it's curious how you get a sense of travel to strange lands in going to some field less than a mile from your home. And you get the feeling of returning from a long exile when you revisit some field that you had walked through as a child....

The village of my native place is built around a disused graveyard. In that graveyard stands a somewhat stunted Round Tower. Liveliest spot in the village is that graveyard. The nettles and weeds are in blossom....

Ah, well, times change and we change with them. Do times really change? I am not so sure. We change. Thinking back into my youth, I know I am occupying another body with a soul that is not quite the same. I am not so innocent now. I have learned to desire, and that is unwisdom....

STONY GREY SOIL

O stony grey soil of Monaghan,
The laugh from my love you thieved;
You took the gay child of my passion
And gave me your clod-conceived.

You clogged the feet of my boyhood,
And I believed that my stumble
Had the poise and stride of Apollo
And his voice my thick-tongued mumble.

You told me the plough was immortal!
O green-life-conquering plough!
Your mandril strained, your coulter blunted
In the smooth lea-field of my brow.

You sang on steaming dunghills
A song of cowards' brood,
You perfumed my clothes with weasel itch,
You fed me on swinish food.

You flung a ditch on my vision
Of beauty, love and truth.
O stony grey soil of Monaghan,
You burgled my bank of youth!

Lost the long hours of pleasure,
All the women that love young men.
O can I still stroke the monster's back
Or write with unpoisoned pen

His name in these lonely verses,
Or mention the dark fields where
The first gay flight of my lyric
Got caught in a peasant's prayer.

Mullahinsha, Drummeril, Black Shanco –
Wherever I turn I see
In the stony grey soil of Monaghan
Dead loves that were born for me.

ADDRESS TO AN OLD WOODEN GATE

Battered by time and weather, scarcely fit
For firewood; there's not a single bit
Of paint to hide those wrinkles, and such
    scringes
Break hoarsely on the silence – rusty hinges:
A barbed wire clasp around one withered arm
Replaces the old latch, with evil charm.
That poplar tree you hang upon is rotten,
And all its early loveliness forgotten.
This gap ere long must find another sentry
If the cows are not to roam the open country.
They'll laugh at you, Old Wooden Gate, they'll
    push
Your limbs asunder, soon, into the slush.
Then I will lean upon your top no more
To muse, and dream of pebbles on a shore,

Or watch the fairy-columned turf-smoke rise
From white-washed cottage chimneys heaven-
    wise.
Here have I kept fair tryst, and kept it true,
When we were lovers all, and you were new;
And many a time I've seen the laughing-eyed
Schoolchildren, on your trusty back astride.
But Time's long silver hand has touched our
    brows,
And I'm the scorned of women – you of cows.
How can I love the iron gates which guard
The fields of wealthy farmers? They are hard,
Unlovely things, a-swing on concrete piers –
Their finger-tips are pointed like old spears.
But you and I are kindred, Ruined Gate,
For both of us have met the self-same fate.

TO A CHILD

Child, do not go
Into the dark places of soul,
For there the grey wolves whine,
The lean grey wolves.

I have been down
Among the unholy ones who tear
Beauty's white robe and clothe her
In rags of prayer.

Child, there is light somewhere
Under a star.
Sometime it will be for you
A window that looks
Inward to God.

BEECH TREE

I planted in February
A bronze-leafed beech,
In the chill brown soil
I spread out its silken fibres.

Protected it from the goats
With wire netting,
And fixed it firm against
The worrying wind.

Now it is safe, I said,
April must stir
My precious baby
To greenful loveliness.

It is August now, I have hoped,
But I hope no more –
My beech tree will never hide sparrows
From hungry hawks.

MONAGHAN HILLS

Monaghan hills,
You have made me the sort of man I am,
A fellow who can never care a damn
For Everestic thrills.

The country of my mind
Has a hundred little heads,
On none of which foot-room for genius.

Because of you I am a half-faithed ploughman,
Shallow furrows at my heels,
Because of you I am a beggar of song
And a coward in thunder.

If I had been born among the Mournes,
Even in Forkhill,
I might have had echo-corners in my soul
Repeating the dawn laughter.

I might have climbed to know the glory
Of toppling from the roof of seeing –
O Monaghan hills, when is writ your story,
A carbon-copy will unfold my being.

PLOUGHMAN

I turn the lea-green down
Gaily now,
And paint the meadow brown
With my plough.

I dream with silvery gull
And brazen crow.
A thing that is beautiful
I may know.

Tranquillity walks with me
And no care.
O, the quiet ecstasy
Like a prayer.

I find a star-lovely art
In a dark sod.
Joy that is timeless! O heart
That knows God!

The Hired Boy

Let me be no wiser than the dull
And leg-dragged boy who wrought
For John Maguire in Donaghmoyne
With never a vain thought
For fortune waiting round the next
Blind turning of Life's lane;
In dreams he never married a lady
To be dreamed-divorced again.

He knew what he wanted to know –
How the best potatoes are grown
And how to put flesh on a York pig's back
And clay on a hilly bone.
And how to be satisfied with the little
The destiny masters give
To the beasts of the tillage country –
To be damned and yet to live.

SHANCODUFF

My black hills have never seen the sun rising,
Eternally they look north towards Armagh.
Lot's wife would not be salt if she had been
Incurious as my black hills that are happy
When dawn whitens Glassdrummond chapel.

My hills hoard the bright shillings of March
While the sun searches in every pocket.
They are my Alps and I have climbed the Matterhorn
With a sheaf of hay for three perishing calves
In the field under the Big Forth of Rocksavage.

The sleety winds fondle the rushy beards of Shancoduff
While the cattle-drovers sheltering in the Featherna Bush
Look up and say: 'Who owns them hungry hills
That the water-hen and snipe must have forsaken?
A poet? Then by heavens he must be poor.'
I hear and is my heart not badly shaken?

SPRAYING THE POTATOES

The barrels of blue potato-spray
Stood on a headland of July
Beside an orchard wall where roses
Were young girls hanging from the sky.

The flocks of green potato-stalks
Were blossom spread for sudden flight,
The Kerr's Pinks in a frivelled blue,
The Arran Banners wearing white.

And over that potato-field
A lazy veil of woven sun.
Dandelions growing on headlands, showing
Their unloved hearts to everyone.

And I was there with the knapsack sprayer
On the barrel's edge poised. A wasp was floating
Dead on a sunken briar leaf
Over a copper-poisoned ocean.

The axle-roll of a rut-locked cart
Broke the burnt stick of noon in two.
An old man came through a corn-field
Remembering his youth and some Ruth he
    knew.

He turned my way. 'God further the work.'
He echoed an ancient farming prayer.
I thanked him. He eyed the potato-drills.
He said: 'You are bound to have good ones
    there.'

We talked and our talk was a theme of kings,
A theme for strings. He hunkered down
In the shade of the orchard wall. O roses,
The old man dies in the young girl's frown.

And poet lost to potato-fields,
Remembering the lime and copper smell
Of the spraying barrels he is not lost
Or till blossomed stalks cannot weave a spell.

Inniskeen Road: July Evening

The bicycles go by in twos and threes –
There's a dance in Billy Brennan's barn tonight,
And there's the half-talk code of mysteries
And the wink-and-elbow language of delight.
Half-past eight and there is not a spot
Upon a mile of road, no shadow thrown
That might turn out a man or woman, not
A footfall tapping secrecies of stone.

I have what every poet hates in spite
Of all the solemn talk of contemplation.
Oh, Alexander Selkirk knew the plight
Of being king and government and nation.
A road, a mile of kingdom, I am king
Of banks and stones and every blooming thing.

from THE LONG GARDEN

It was the garden of the golden apples,
A long garden between a railway and a road,
In the sow's rooting where the hen scratches
We dipped our fingers in the pockets of God.

In the thistly hedge old boots were flying sandals
By which we travelled through the childhood skies,
Old buckets rusty-holed with half-hung handles
Were drums to play when old men married wives.

The pole that lifted the clothes-line in the middle
Was the flag-pole on a prince's palace when
We looked at it through fingers crossed to riddle
In evening sunlight miracles for men.

It was the garden of the golden apples,
And when the Carrick train went by we knew
That we could never die till something happened,
Like wishing for a fruit that never grew....

from LIVING IN THE COUNTRY

Opening

It was the Warm Summer, that landmark
In a child's mind, an infinite day,
Sunlight and burnt grass,
Green grasshoppers on the railway slopes,
The humming of wild bees,
The whole summer during the school holidays
Till the blackberries appeared.
Yes, a tremendous time that summer stands
Beyond the grey finities of normal weather.

The Main Body

It's not nearly as bad as you'd imagine
Living among small farmers in the north of
    Ireland.
They are for the most part the ordinary
    frightened,
Blind brightened, referred to sometimes socially
As the underprivileged.
They cannot perceive Irony or even Satire;
They start up with insane faces if
You break the newspaper moral code....

There's little you can do about some
Who roar horribly as you enter a bar
Incantations of ugliness, words of half a syllable,
Locked in malicious muteness full of glare.
And your dignity thinks of giving up the beer.
But I, trained in the slum pubs of Dublin
Among the most offensive class of all –
The artisans – am equal to this problem;
I let it ride and there is nothing over.
I understand through all these years
That my difference in their company is an
    intrusion
That tears at the sentimental clichés;
They can see my heart squirm when their star
    rendites
The topmost twenty in the lowered lights.
No, sir, I did not come unprepared....

WHY SORROW? [a fragment]

...
His hand upon the dash-board of a cart,
Father Mat was standing
Talking to Michael Duffy about fairs,
The price of pigs and store-cattle –
Like a dealer in the Shercock fair bawling in the doorways of shops.
His heavy hat was square upon his head
Like a Christian Brother's,
His eyes were watery like an old man's eyes,
And out of his flat nose grew spiky hairs.
Michael Duffy wondered as he saw him thus:
So like mere earth and yet not one of us.

                    It was the gap
Between the seasons, and the days moved slowly,
With labouring men sleeping on headlands among the nettles
And long arms hooked over gates that brightened
The gravel patches on the June road.
The priest spoke wistfully, rurally, heavily,
And no one could know that he was seeing
Down the shaft of the gate's light, horses growing wings;
The midges caught in the searchlight
Were beautiful, unChristian things....

from A CHRISTMAS CHILDHOOD

II

My father played the melodion
Outside at our gate;
There were stars in the morning east
And they danced to his music.

Across the wild bogs his melodion called
To Lennons and Callans.
As I pulled on my trousers in a hurry
I knew some strange thing had happened.

Outside in the cow-house my mother
Made the music of milking;
The light of her stable-lamp was a star
And the frost of Bethlehem made it twinkle.

A water-hen screeched in the bog,
Mass-going feet
Crunched the wafer-ice on the pot-holes,
Somebody wistfully twisted the bellows wheel.

My child poet picked out the letters
On the grey stone,
In silver the wonder of a Christmas townland,
The winking glitter of a frosty dawn.

Cassiopeia was over
Cassidy's hanging hill,
I looked and three whin bushes rode across
The horizon – the Three Wise Kings.

An old man passing said:
'Can't he make it talk –
The melodion.' I hid in the doorway
And tightened the belt of my box-pleated coat.

I nicked six nicks on the door-post
With my penknife's big blade –
There was a little one for cutting tobacco.
And I was six Christmases of age.

My father played the melodion,
My mother milked the cows,
And I had a prayer like a white rose pinned
On the Virgin Mary's blouse.

CHRISTMAS EVE REMEMBERED

I see them going to the chapel
To confess their sins. Christmas Eve
In a parish in Monaghan.
Poor parish! and yet memory does weave
For me about those folk
A romantic cloak.

No snow, but in their minds
The fields and roads are white;
They may be talking of the turkey markets
Or foreign politics, but to-night
Their plain, hard country words
Are Christ's singing birds.

Bicycles scoot by. Old women
Cling to the grass margin:
Their thoughts are earthy, but their minds move
In dreams of the Blessed Virgin,
For One in Bethlehem
Has kept their dreams safe for them

'Did you hear from Tom this Christmas?'
'These are the dark days.'
'Maguire's shop did a great trade,
Turnover double – so Maguire says.'
'I can't delay now, Jem,
Lest I be late in Bethlehem.'

Like this my memory saw,
Like this my childhood heard
These pilgrims of the North…
And memory you have me spared
A light to follow them
Who go to Bethlehem.

LOVE IN A MEADOW

She waved her body in the circle sign
Of love purely born without side;
The earth's contour she orbited to my pride,
Sin and unsin.
But the critic asking questions ran
From the fright of the dawn
To weep later on an urban lawn
For the undone
God-gifted man.
O the river flowed round and round
The low meadows filled with buttercups
In a place called Toprass.
I was born on high ground.

PEACE

And sometimes I am sorry when the grass
Is growing over the stones in quiet hollows
And the cocksfoot leans across the rutted cart-pass,
That I am not the voice of country fellows
Who now are standing by some headland talking
Of turnips and potatoes or young corn
Or turf banks stripped for victory.
Here Peace is still hawking
His coloured combs and scarves and beads of horn.

Upon a headland by a whinny hedge
A hare sits looking down a leaf-lapped furrow;
There's an old plough upside-down on a weedy ridge
And someone is shouldering home a saddle-harrow.
Out of that childhood country what fools climb
To fight with tyrants Love and Life and Time?

PART 2

FROM INNISKEEN
TO DUBLIN:
'THE SIMPLICITY
OF GOING AWAY...'

'Curious this, how I had started off with

the right simplicity, indifferent to crude

reason, and then ploughed my way through

complexities and anger, hatred and ill-will

towards the faults of man, and came back to

where I started.'

Self-Portrait

Kavanagh's early years in Dublin have been variously interpreted. He was a countryman, a small farmer, newly arrived in the city – or, less kindly, an unkempt difficult peasant farmer. He had been to Dublin many times before 1939. This time he walked the sixty miles from Inniskeen to meet the writer Æ, who was not expecting him. He was not dressed appropriately and was acutely self-conscious of his attire in the company of writers. He wasn't playing up the archetypal rural peasant, nor was he flouting social etiquette. He simply had no place in Dublin society, nor in London.

The myths and misrepresentations grew. The latest episode involving Kavanagh became part of Dublin literary gossip: a row at a bar or the dismissal of a politician, an artist, a would-be poet or others who regarded themselves as established.

The stories about Kavanagh and his tormentor, Brendan Behan, are legion. Behan was mean-spirited when drunk, loud, brawling and with an equally mean retinue. Kavanagh genuinely feared the younger playwright. Their confrontations did, however, provide some amusement. During his secondary school years at Blackrock College, Brian O'Nolan (Myles na gCopaleen) was a pupil of Archbishop McQuaid and took pleasure in imitating his 'finicky' handwriting. There was great hilarity when Kavanagh accidentally dropped a note from McQuaid in a pub, and Behan picked it up and mockingly read it out. Behan and a friend, Sean Daly, would try to get a rise out of Kavanagh by playing ritual scenes of Kavanagh kissing McQuaid's ring. 'Oh, the Archbishop is not such an ould bastard,' Kavanagh responded.[2]

Little came easy for the poet. He was very insecure for many years and employment was fleeting. Journalism rather than poetry kept him going. Patrick's brother, Peter, had trained as a national teacher at St Patrick's Training College, Drumcondra, qualifying in 1936. This was a significant achievement since it would eventually put him in a position to support his brother. It wasn't until he and his brother Peter settled in Pembroke Road that Kavanagh was able to establish a routine. He wrote in the morning and the rest of the day was spent in various locales depending on where he found work. He made a modest amount from book reviewing, usually ten shillings per review. His usual practice was to sell the book to Greene's of Clare Street. He didn't always get the one-third of the list price that he asked for.

BAGGOT STREET AND PEMBROKE ROAD

According to Benedict Kiely: 'Baggot Street if you look at it has all the characteristics of a street in a country town: it even has a bridge at the end of it, small shops, everything Paddy needed to make him feel he was walking up and down Carrickmacross on a market day.'[3]

Pembroke Road was a tree-lined Victorian thoroughfare, and led into the end of Baggot Street, which had a handful of pubs, a bookmaker's shop and a bookshop. Anthony Cronin wrote:

This was his querencia. Here he prowled, newspapers under one arm, eyes baleful behind horn-rimmed glasses, the enormous hands projecting behind each elbow, hat on head. Often as he walked he talked to himself or, scowling, muttered at the ground. In the local pubs he was well known to all and sundry, and he conversed with everyone whether they would or no, but usually with their consent, for he had views and knowledge on everything, the more trivial the better.

Seldom can there have been such a small area so patrolled by genius: every gurrier in Kilmartin's the bookies, every dart playing docker in Tommy Ryan's, every gin-drinking landlady or middle-class soak in the Waterloo Lounge was known to him. The girls in the shops and the students and the typists who had flats in Pembroke Road he conversed with; indeed he held curious flirtations with many of them, which were nonetheless intense for being merely a matter of street-corner conversation, often mystifying to the girls, about matters ranging from their progress in examinations to the persecutions he suffered.'[4]

Kavanagh was a very visible presence in Dublin, later on more so because of the notoriety he gained during the libel case. When he wasn't writing or passing time in the pubs, he walked, cycled or took a bus on his travels. John McGahern, the novelist and short-story writer, creates a haunting image of Kavanagh in a pub:

> Soon in the drowsiness of the stout, we did little but watch others drinking. I pointed out a poet to her. I recognised him from his pictures in the paper. His shirt was open-necked inside a gabardine coat and he wore a hat with a small feather in its band....Four men at the table continually plied him with whiskey. He was saying he loved the blossoms of Kerr Pinks more than roses, a man could only love what he knew well, and it was the quality of the love that mattered and not the accident. The whole table said they'd drink to that, but he glared at them as if slighted, and as if to avoid the glare they called for a round of doubles.[5]

Notes

1. Quoted in Bevis Hiller, *John Betjeman: New Fame, New Love* (London, 2002), p. 218.

2. Benedict Kiely, RTE Archives, 'Jungle of Pembroke Road,' 6 October 1974.

3. Anthony Cronin, *Dead as Doornails*, p. 75.

4. John McGahern, 'My Love, My Umbrella', in *Creatures of the Earth* (Faber and Faber, 2006), p. 60.

Europe Is at War – Remembering Its Pastoral Peace

Midnight in Dublin. A wild, but not cold October wind is driving rain against my window. The last buses are swishing by on the glassy-bright streets. The radio in the flat above me has stopped forwarding to this address the mixture of blather and jazz which is called propaganda....

Being an Irishman I should be abnormal if I didn't dream, think and write of far-past peace and quiet in pastoral fields when everybody else is thinking in terms of war.

And just now I remember. Oh, no, I see. In the mirror of this mood I see....

An October evening in a country place. A small farmhouse among leaf-lamenting poplars. In a garden before the house men are pitting potatoes. A cart is heeled up. Two men are working at the back of the cart unloading the potatoes with their muddy hands, while a boy with a stable lamp stands by the horse's head.

The horse snaps at the top of a tall, withered thistle....

There is the rumble of heavy-laden carts passing along the little road.

In the mirror those rugged men sitting high on their loads of potatoes and potato stalks become figures of romantic allure, sculptures pedestalled in the mud-walled temples of rural Ireland....

And the carts rumble on while the poplars continue to lament. Poplars, the banshees of the forest....

For a moment I avert my gaze from the mirror of memory, and am again aware of Dublin and the last blue-lit ghostbus passing. I remember some wild talk of a war in Europe.... the radio commentator. But I know that beyond the headlines, beneath the contemporary froth and flurry, the tide of humanity flows calm.

And was I once part of this simple, deep life? Did I once experience the joy of being one of those people, part of that experience? The joy of it. Stark and lonely it might seem at times, grey and forlorn as the night poplars of late autumn, but it was real life among real folk, without the fake conventions that put gilt on tin-pot souls. No highfalutin culture.

Cruel and vulgar those folk might be at times or vexingly peasant-deceitful, but there was in them in a greater or lesser degree something of the sensitivity which is part of the poet's misery – an unprotected heart.

It is midnight in Dublin and Europe is at war.

JIM LARKIN

Not with public words now can his greatness
Be told to the children, for he was more
Than a labour-agitating orator –
The flashing flaming sword merely bore witness
To the coming of the dawn. 'Awake and look!
The flowers are growing for you, and wonderful trees,
And beyond are not the serf's grey docks, but seas –
Excitement out of the creator's poetry book.
When the Full Moon's in the River the ghost of bread
Must not haunt all your weary wanderings home.
The ships that were dark galleys can become
Pine forests under the winter's starry plough
And the brown gantries will be the lifted hand
Of man the dreamer whom the gods endow.'
And thus I hear Jim Larkin shout above
The crowd who wanted to turn aside
From Reality coming to free them. Terrified,
They hid in the clouds of dope and would not move.
They ate the opium of the murderer's story
In the Sunday newspapers; they stood to stare
Not at a blackbird, but a millionaire
Whose horses ran for serfdom's greater glory.
And Tyranny trampled them in Dublin's gutter,
Until Larkin came along and cried
The call of Freedom and the call of Pride,
And Slavery crept to its hands and knees,
And Nineteen Thirteen cheered from out the utter
Degradation of their miseries.

from A WREATH FOR TOM MOORE'S STATUE

The cowardice of Ireland is in his statue,
No poet's honoured when they wreathe this stone,
An old shopkeeper who has dealt in the marrow-bone
Of his neighbours looks at you.
Dim-eyed, degenerate, he is admiring his god,
The bank-manager who pays his monthly confession,
The tedious narrative of a mediocrity's passion,
The shallow, safe sins that never become a flood
To sweep themselves away. From under
His coat-lapels the vermin creep as Joyce
Noted in passing on his exile's way.
In the wreathing of this stone now I wonder
If there is not somehow the worship of the lice
That crawl upon the seven-deadened clay.

They put a wreath upon the dead
For the dead will wear the cap of any racket,
The corpse will not put his elbows through his jacket
Or contradict the words some liar has said.
The corpse can be fitted out to deceive –
Fake thoughts, false love, fake ideal,
And rogues can sell its guaranteed appeal,
Guaranteed to work and never come alive.
The poet would not stay poetical
And his humility was far from being pliable,
Voluptuary tomorrow, today ascetical,
His morning gentleness was the evening's rage....

ON RAGLAN ROAD

On Raglan Road on an autumn day I met her first and knew
That her dark hair would weave a snare that I might one day rue;
I saw the danger, yet I walked along the enchanted way,
And I said, let grief be a fallen leaf at the dawning of the day.

On Grafton street in November we tripped lightly along the ledge
Of the deep ravine where can be seen the worth of passion's pledge,
The Queen of Hearts still making tarts and I not making hay –
O I loved too much and by such, by such, is happiness thrown away.

I gave her gifts of the mind, I gave her the secret sign that's known
To the artists who have known the true gods of sound and stone
And word and tint. I did not stint for I gave her poems to say
With her own name there and her own dark hair like clouds over fields of May.

On a quiet street where old ghosts meet I see her walking now
Away from me so hurriedly my reason must allow
That I had wooed not as I should a creature made of clay –
When the angel woos the clay he'd lose his wings at the dawn of day.

from THE GREAT HUNGER

I

Clay is the word and clay is the flesh
Where the potato-gatherers like mechanized
    scare-crows move
Along the side-fall of the hill – Maguire and
    his men.
If we watch them an hour is there anything we
    can prove
Of life as it is broken-backed over the Book
Of Death? Here crows gabble over worms and
    frogs
And the gulls like old newspapers are blown
    clear of the hedges, luckily.
Is there some light of imagination in these wet
    clods?
Or why do we stand here shivering?
                    Which of these men
Loved the light and the queen
Too long virgin? Yesterday was summer. Who
    was it promised marriage to himself
Before apples were hung from the ceilings for
    Hallowe'en?
We will wait and watch the tragedy to the last
    curtain,
Till the last soul passively like a bag of wet clay

Rolls down the side of the hill, diverted by the
    angles
Where the plough missed or a spade stands,
    straitening the way.
A dog lying on a torn jacket under a heeled-up
    cart,
A horse nosing along the posied headland,
    trailing
A rusty plough. Three heads hanging between
    wide-apart
Legs. October playing a symphony on a slack
    wire paling.
Maguire watches the drills flattened out
And the flints that lit a candle for him on a
    June altar
Flameless. The drills slipped by and the days
    slipped by
And he trembled his head away and ran free
    from the world's halter,
And thought himself wiser than any man in
    the townland
When he laughed over pints of porter
Of how he came free from every net spread
In the gaps of experience. He shook a knowing
    head
And pretended to his soul
That children are tedious in hurrying fields of
    April

Where men are spanging across wide furrows,
Lost in the passion that never needs a wife –
The pricks that pricked were the pointed pins
    of harrows.
Children scream so loud that the crows could
    bring
The seed of an acre away with crow-rude jeers.
Patrick Maguire, he called his dog and he flung
    a stone in the air
And hallooed the birds away that were the
    birds of the years.
Turn over the weedy clods and tease out the
    tangled skeins.
What is he looking for there?
He thinks it is a potato, but we know better
Than his mud-gloved fingers probe in this
    insensitive hair....

            II
Maguire was faithful to death:
He stayed with his mother till she died
At the age of ninety-one.
She stayed too long,
Wife and mother in one.
When she died
The knuckle-bones were cutting the skin of her
    son's backside
And he was sixty-five.

O he loved his mother
Above all others.
O he loved his ploughs
And he loved his cows
And his happiest dream
Was to clean his arse
With perennial grass
On the bank of some summer stream;
To smoke his pipe
In a sheltered gripe
In the middle of July –
His face in a mist
And two stones in his fist
And an impotent worm on his thigh.

But his passion became a plague
For he grew feeble bringing the vague
Women of his mind to lust nearness,
Once a week at least flesh must make an
    appearance.

So Maguire got tired
Of the no-target gun fired
And returned to his headlands of carrots and
    cabbage.
To the fields once again
Where eunuchs can be men
And life is more lousy than savage.

VII

'Now go to Mass and pray and confess your
    sins
And you'll have all the luck,' his mother said.
He listened to the lie that is a woman's screen
Around a conscience when soft thighs are
    spread.
And all the while she was setting up the lie
She trusted in Nature that never deceives.
But her son took it as the literal truth.
Religion's walls expand to the push of nature.
    Morality yields
To sense – but not in little tillage fields….

XI

A year passed and another hurried after it
And Patrick Maguire was still six months
    behind life –
His mother six months ahead of it;
His sister straddle-legged across it: –
One leg in hell and the other in heaven
And between the purgatory of middle-aged
    virginity –
She prayed for release to heaven or hell.
His mother's voice grew thinner like a rust-
    worn knife
But it cut more venomously as it thinned,
It cut him up the middle till he became more
    woman than man,

And it cut through to his mind before the
    end….

XIV

…
Maguire is not afraid of death, the Church will
    light him a candle
To see his way through the vaults and he'll
    understand the
Quality of the clay that dribbles over his coffin.
He'll know the names of the roots that climb
    down to tickle his feet.
And he will feel no different than when he
    walked through Donaghmoyne.
If he stretches out a hand – a wet clod,
If he opens his nostrils – a dungy smell;
If he opens his eyes once in a million years –
Through a crack in the crust of the earth he
    may see a face nodding in
Or a woman's legs. Shut them again for that
    sight is sin….

He stands in the doorway of his house
A ragged sculpture of the wind,
October creaks the rotted mattress,
The bedposts fall. No hope. No lust.
The hungry fiend
Screams the apocalypse of clay
In every corner of this land.

OCTOBER 1943

And the rain coming down, and the rain coming down!
How lovely it falls on the rick well headed,
On potato pits thatched, on the turf clamps home,
On the roofs of the byre where the cows are bedded!

And the sun shining down, and the sun shining down!
How bright on the turnip leaves, on the stubble –
Where turkeys tip-toe across the ridges –
In this corner of peace in a world of trouble.

KERR'S ASS

We borrowed the loan of Kerr's big ass
To go to Dundalk with butter,
Brought him home the evening before the market
An exile that night in Mucker.

We heeled up the cart before the door,
We took the harness inside –
The straw-stuffed straddle, the broken breeching
With bits of bull-wire tied;

The winkers that had no choke-band,
The collar and the reins…
In Ealing Broadway, London Town,
I name their several names

Until a world comes to life –
Morning, the silent bog,
And the god of imagination waking
In a Mucker fog.

from TARRY FLYNN

The division between this field and the portion of the farm which ran down the other side of the hill was a clay bank upon which yellow-blossomed whins grew. Flinging his jacket across the fence he walked back a few steps and took a race to the fence to see if he could leap it. His second love had always been athletics and on summer mornings he was usually to be seen running in his stockinged feet round the home farm, over hedges and drains and palings.

He leaped on to the fence among the whins and found himself standing above the world of Drumnay and Miskin and looking far into the east where the dark fields of Cavan fanned out through a gap in the hills into the green fertile plains of Louth.

The rain had stopped and the sun was coming out and the bees and stinging clags were coming alive again.

MEMORY OF MY FATHER

Every old man I see
Reminds me of my father
When he had fallen in love with death
One time when sheaves were gathered.

That man I saw in Gardiner Street
Stumble on the kerb was one,
He stared at me half-eyed,
I might have been his son.

And I remember the musician
Faltering over his fiddle
In Bayswater, London,
He too set me the riddle.

Every old man I see
In October-coloured weather
Seems to say to me:
'I was once your father.'

from THE POET'S READY RECKONER

...

In the disused railway siding
(O railway that came up from Enniskillen)
A new living is spreading,
Dandelions that grow from wagon-grease.
I stand on the platform
And peace, perfect peace,
Descends on me....

In Memory of My Mother

I do not think of you lying in the wet clay
Of a Monaghan graveyard; I see
You walking down a lane among the poplars
On your way to the station, or happily

Going to second Mass on a summer Sunday –
You meet me and you say:
'Don't forget to see about the cattle –'
Among your earthiest words the angels stray.

And I think of you walking along a headland
Of green oats in June,
So full of repose, so rich with life –
And I see us meeting at the end of a town

On a fair day by accident, after
The bargains are all made and we can walk
Together through the shops and stalls and markets
Free in the oriental streets of thought.

O you are not lying in the wet clay,
For it is a harvest evening now and we
Are piling up the ricks against the moonlight
And you smile up at us – eternally.

Winter

Christmas, someone mentioned, is almost upon us
And looking out my window I saw that Winter had landed
Complete with the grey cloud and the bare tree sonnet,
A scroll of bark hanging down to the knees as he scanned it.
The gravel in the yard was pensive, annoyed to be crunched
As people with problems in their faces drove by in cars,
Yet I with such solemnity around me refused to be bunched,
In fact was inclined to give the go-by to bars.
Yes, there were things in that winter arrival that made me
Feel younger, less of a failure, it was actually earlier
Than many people thought; there were possibilities
For love, for South African adventure, for fathering a baby,
For taking oneself in hand, catching on without a scare me, or
Taking part in a world war, joing up at the start of hostilities.

IRISH POETS OPEN YOUR EYES

Irish poets open your eyes,
Even Cabra can surprise;
Try the dog-tracks now and then –
Shelbourne Park and crooked men.

Could you ever pray at all
In the Pro-Cathedral
Till a breath of simpleness
Freed your Freudian distress?

Enter in and be a part
Of the world's frustrated heart,
Drive the golf ball of despair,
Superdance away your care.

Be ordinary,
Be saving up to marry.
Kiss her in the alleyway,
Part – 'Same time, same place' – and go.

Learn repose on Boredom's bed,
Deep, anonymous, unread,
And the god of Literature
Will touch a moment to endure.

IF EVER YOU GO TO DUBLIN TOWN

If ever you go to Dublin town
In a hundred years or so
Inquire for me in Baggot Street
And what I was like to know.
O he was a queer one
Fol dol the di do,
He was a queer one
I tell you.

My great-grandmother knew him well,
He asked her to come and call
On him in his flat and she giggled at the thought
Of a young girl's lovely fall.
O he was dangerous
Fol dol the di do,
He was dangerous
I tell you.

On Pembroke Road look out for my ghost
Dishevelled with shoes untied,
Playing through the railings with little children
Whose children have long since died.
O he was a nice man
Fol dol the di do,
He was a nice man
I tell you.

Go into a pub and listen well
If my voice still echoes there,
Ask the men what their grandsires thought
And tell them to answer fair.
O he was eccentric
Fol dol the di do,
He was eccentric
I tell you.

He had the knack of making men feel
As small as they really were
Which meant as great as God had made them
But as males they disliked his air.
O he was a proud one
Fol dol the di do,
He was a proud one
I tell you.

If ever you go to Dublin town
In a hundred years or so,
Sniff for my personality,
Is it vanity's vapour now?
O he was a vain one
Fol dol the di do,
He was a vain one
I tell you.

I saw his name with a hundred others
In a book in the library;
It said he had never fully achieved
His potentiality.
O he was slothful
Fol dol the di do
He was slothful
I tell you.

He knew that posterity has no use
For anything but the soul,
The lines that speak the passionate heart,
The spirit that lives alone.
O he was a lone one
Fol dol the di do,
Yet he lived happily
I tell you.

CONSIDER THE GRASS GROWING

Consider the grass growing
As it grew last year and the year before,
Cool about the ankles like summer rivers,
When we walked on a May evening through the meadows
To watch the mare that was going to foal.

Leaves of Grass

When I was growing up and for many years after
I was led to believe that poems were thin,
Dreary, irrelevant, well out of the draught of laughter,
With headquarters the size of the head of a pin.
I do not wonder now that my mother moaned
To see her beloved son an idiot boy;
He could not see what was before his eyes, the ground
Tumultuous with living, infinite as Cleopatra's variety.
He hit upon the secret door that leads to the heaven
Of human satisfaction, a purpose, and did not know it;
An army of grass blades were at his call, million on million
Kept saying to him, we nearly made Whitman a poet.
Years after in Dublin in summer past midnight o'clock
They called to him vainly from kerbstones on Bachelor's Walk.

I HAD A FUTURE

O I had a future,
A future.

Gods of the imagination bring back to life
The personality of those streets,
Not any streets
But the streets of nineteen-forty.

Give the quarter-seeing eyes I looked out of,
The animal-remembering mind,
The fog through which I walked towards the mirage
That was my future.

The women I was to meet,
They were nowhere within sight.

And then the pathos of the blind soul,
Who without knowing stands in its own kingdom.

Bring me a small detail
How I felt about money,
Not frantic as later,
There was the future.

Show me the stretcher-bed I slept on
In a room on Drumcondra Road.
Let John Betjeman call for me in a car.

It is summer and the eerie beat
Of madness in Europe trembles the
Wings of the butterflies along the canal.

O I had a future.

THE ROWLEY MILE

As I was walking down a street
Upon a summer's day
A typical girl I chanced to meet
And gathered courage to say:
'I've seen you many, many times
Upon this Rowley Mile
And I'm foolish enough to believe you love
Me for you always smile.'

Well, she gathered herself into a ball
Receding all the time.
She said: 'I beg your pardon,
I do not know what you mean.'
I stammered vainly for the right word,
I said: 'I mean to say
I'm not trying to get off with you
Or anything in that way.'

The street was full of eyes that stared
At something very odd.
I tried to imagine how little means
Such a contretemps to God.
I followed her a few slow yards,
'Please just one moment stop',
And then I dashed with urgent tread
Into a corner shop.

As I walked down that sunny street
I was a broken man
Thanks to an Irish girl
Who smiles but is true to the plan
Taught her by Old Gummy Granny –
You must try out your power with a smile,
But come to the test hard reality must
Make the pace on the Rowley Mile.

Who Killed James Joyce?

Who killed James Joyce?
I, said the commentator,
I killed James Joyce
For my graduation.

What weapon was used
To slay mighty Ulysses?
The weapon that was used
Was a Harvard thesis.

How did you bury Joyce?
In a broadcast Symposium,
That's how we buried Joyce
To a tuneful encomium.

Who carried the coffin out?
Six Dublin codgers
Led into Langham Place
By W.R. Rodgers.

Who said the burial prayers? –
Please do not hurt me –
Joyce was no Protestant,
Surely not Bertie?

Who killed Finnegan?
I, said a Yale-man,
I was the man who made
The corpse for the wake man.

And did you get high marks,
The Ph.D.?
I got the B. Litt.
And my master's degree.

Did you get money
For your Joycean knowledge?
I got a scholarship
To Trinity College.

I made the pilgrimage
In the Bloomsday swelter
From the Martello Tower
To the cabby's shelter.

from TALE OF TWO CITIES

The streets of London are not paved with gold,
The streets of London are paved with failures;
They get up and move about when they are filled with drink,
Just as in Dublin. Yesterday in Fleet Street
In a pub I met one. He shook my hand
And he was full of poisonous good fellowship as he looked into
　　my eyes:
I would have a double whiskey.
I was from Dublin, most wonderful spot on earth….

I'll tell you the name of the greatest living poet, he muttered,
He lives near Manchester and will be heard of yet.
What about Auden? I interrupted. He ignored me –
Yeats was second-rate, not a patch on Higgins –
I was back in Dublin as I listened….

INNOCENCE

They laughed at one I loved –
The triangular hill that hung
Under the Big Forth. They said
That I was bounded by the whitethorn hedges
Of the little farm and did not know the world.
But I knew that love's doorway to life
Is the same doorway everywhere.

Ashamed of what I loved
I flung her from me and called her a ditch
Although she was smiling at me with violets.

But now I am back in her briary arms;
The dew of an Indian Summer morning lies
On bleached potato-stalks –
What age am I?

I do not know what age I am,
I am no mortal age;
I know nothing of women,
Nothing of cities,
I cannot die
Unless I walk outside these whitethorn hedges.

EPIC

I have lived in important places, times
When great events were decided: who owned
That half a rood of rock, a no-man's land
Surrounded by our pitchfork-armed claims.
I heard the Duffys shouting 'Damn your soul'
And old McCabe, stripped to the waist, seen
Step the plot defying blue cast-steel –
'Here is the march along these iron stones.'
That was the year of the Munich bother. Which
Was most important? I inclined
To lose my faith in Ballyrush and Gortin
Till Homer's ghost came whispering to my mind.
He said: I made the *Iliad* from such
A local row. Gods make their own importance.

WET EVENING IN APRIL

The birds sang in the wet trees
And as I listened to them it was a hundred years from now
And I was dead and someone else was listening to them.
But I was glad I had recorded for him the melancholy.

The Hospital

A year ago I fell in love with the functional ward
Of a chest hospital: square cubicles in a row,
Plain concrete, wash basins – an art lover's woe,
Not counting how the fellow in the next bed snored.
But nothing whatever is by love debarred,
The common and banal her heat can know.
The corridor led to a stairway and below
Was the inexhaustible adventure of a gravelled yard.

This is what love does to things: the Rialto Bridge,
The main gate that was bent by a heavy lorry,
The seat at the back of a shed that was a suntrap.
Naming these things is the love-act and its pledge;
For we must record love's mystery without claptrap,
Snatch out of time the passionate transitory.

CANAL BANK WALK

Leafy-with-love banks and the green waters of the canal
Pouring redemption for me, that I do
The will of God, wallow in the habitual, the banal,
Grow with nature again as before I grew.
The bright stick trapped, the breeze adding a third
Party to the couple kissing on an old seat,
And a bird gathering materials for the nest for the Word,
Eloquently new and abandoned to its delirious beat.
O unworn world enrapture me, encapture me in a web
Of fabulous grass and eternal voices by a beech,
Feed the gaping need of my senses, give me ad lib
To pray unselfconsciously with overflowing speech,
For this soul needs to be honoured with a new dress woven
From green and blue things and arguments that cannot be proven.

Lines Written on a Seat on the Grand Canal, Dublin
'Erected to the Memory of Mrs. Dermod O'Brien'

O commemorate me where there is water,
Canal water preferably, so stilly
Greeny at the heart of summer. Brother
Commemorate me thus beautifully
Where by a lock Niagarously roars
The falls for those who sit in the tremendous silence
Of mid-July. No one will speak in prose
Who finds his way to these Parnassian islands.
A swan goes by head low with many apologies,
Fantastic light looks through the eyes of bridges –
And look! A barge comes bringing from Athy
And other far-flung towns mythologies.
O commemorate me with no hero-courageous
Tomb – just a canal-bank seat for the passer-by.

A Ballad

O cruel are the women of Dublin's fair city,
They smile out of cars and are gone in a flash,
You know they are charming and gay in their hearts
And would laugh as vivaciously buried in chaff
As they would underneath a pink shower of confetti.

I knew one in Baggot Street, a medical student
Unless I am greatly mistaken is she;
Her smile plays a tune on my trembling psyche
At thirty yards range, but she passes by me
In a frost that would make Casanova be prudent.

It's the same everywhere – the wish without will,
And it tortures, yet I would not change it for all
The women from Bond Street right down to The Mall,
For wealth is potential, not the readies at call,
I say as I walk down from Baggot Street Bridge.

from LITERARY ADVENTURES

I am here in a garage in Monaghan.
It is June and the weather is warm,
Just a little bit cloudy. There's the sun again
Lifting to importance my sixteen acre farm....
Spread this news, tell all if you love me,
You who knew that when sick I was never dying
(Nae gane, nae gane, nae frae us torn
But taking a rest like John Jordan).
                         Other exclusive
News stories that cannot be ignored:
I climbed Woods' Hill and the elusive
Underworld of the grasses could be heard;
John Lennon shouted across the valley.
Then I saw a New June Moon, quite as stunning
As when young we blessed the sight as something holy...
Sensational adventure that is only beginning....

THAT GARAGE

The lilacs by the gate,
The summer sun again,
The swallows in and out
Of the garage where I am.
The sounds of land activity,
Machinery in gear;
This is not longevity
But infinity.
Perhaps a little bit
Too facilely romantic;
We must stop and struggle with
A mood that's going frantic,
Getting Georgian,
Richard Church and Binyon.
O stand and plan
More difficult dominion.

Personal Problem

To take something as a subject, indifferent
To personal affection, I have been considering
Some old saga as an instrument
To play upon without the person suffering
From the tiring years. But I can only
Tell of my problem without solving
Anything. If I could rewrite a famous tale
Or perhaps return to a midnight calving,
This cow sacred on a Hindu scale –
So there it is my friends. What am I to do
With the void growing more awful every hour?
I lacked a classical discipline. I grew
Uncultivated and now the soil turns sour,
Needs to be revived by a power not my own,
Heroes enormous who do astounding deeds –
Out of this world. Only thus can I attune
To despair an illness like winter alone in Leeds.

THANK YOU, THANK YOU

…Particularly if yourself
Have been left as they call it on the shelf,
All God's chillun got wings,
So the black Alabaman sings.

Down Grafton Street on Saturdays
Don't grieve like Marcus Aurelius
Who said that though he grew old and grey
The people on the Appian Way
Were always the same pleasant age,
Twenty-four on average.

I can never help reflecting
On coming back in another century
From now and feeling comfortable
At a buzzing coffee table,
Students in 2056
With all the old eternal tricks.

The thing that I most glory in
Is this exciting, unvarying
Quality that withal
Is completely original.

For what it teaches is just this:
We are not alone in our loneliness;
Others have been here and known
Griefs we thought our special own,
Problems that we could not solve,
Lovers that we could not have,
Pleasures that we missed by inches.
Come I'm beginning to get pretentious,
Beginning to message forth instead
Of expressing how glad
I am to have lived to feel the radiance
Of a holy hearing audience
And delivered God's commands
Into those caressing hands,
My personality that's to say
All that is mine exclusively.
What wisdom's ours if such there be
Is a flavour of personality.
I thank you and I say how proud
That I have been by fate allowed
To stand here having the joyful chance
To claim my inheritance,
For most have died the day before
The opening of that holy door.

NOTES

Page

19 'Some Evocations of No Importance' was published in *Collected Pruse* (London, 1973) pp. 33-41.

20 'Stony Grey Soil': With regard to 'weasel itch', according to UCD folklorist Dáithí Ó hÓgáin: 'In certain parts of the country there was a belief that if you left a coat unattended in the potato field, a weasel might come along and spray it. The stench from this spray was difficult to get rid of, and gave the wearer of the coat the itch.'

29 'Monaghan Hills': Kavanagh's ambivalence about the importance of place in his poetic development is evident here.

31 'Ploughman' was first published in *The Irish Statesman*, the weekly journal edited by Æ, on 15 February 1930. Kavanagh was ploughing in Shancoduff when the poem was accepted for publication. Having his work published in a literary journal was a breakthrough for the poet. Although he later railed against the hardship of small-time farming, he was content at this time. Much of his poetry is spare, direct and simple. 'Ploughman' reflects his passionate love of the land. Kavanagh bought his first copy of *The Irish Statesman* in O'Neill's bookshop, Dundalk. For several months, he would cycle the nine miles to Dundalk to buy this weekly. After his poems started to appear in the journal, Æ sent him a free copy by post each week. 'Ploughman', the first of his country poems, is familiar to generations of Irish schoolchildren.

32 'The Hired Boy' was first published in *Ireland Today* in October 1936.

34 'Shancoduff': Shancoduff, located about half a mile from Kavanagh's house, was purchased in 1926 – the seven fields known as Reynolds's Farm. It is an accurate depiction of the unyielding land. In *Self-Portrait*, Kavanagh commented: 'Thirty years earlier, Shancoduff's watery hills could have done the trick but I was too thick to take the hint. Curious this, how I had started off with the right simplicity, indifferent to crude reason, and then ploughed my way through complexities and anger, hatred and ill-will towards the faults of man, and came back to where I started.'

36 'Spraying the Potatoes': To prevent blight, potatoes had to be sprayed each year with copper sulphate (bluestone) dissolved in water with washing soda. A forty-gallon timber barrel filled with the spray was positioned in a convenient spot in the field's headland and the farmer or workman strapped a two-gallon sprayer on his back. Small farmers rented this equipment. The sprayer walked up and down between the drills, spraying the leaves. It was demanding work and the sprayer often got well soaked in spray.

40 'The Long Garden': The 'Carrick' referred to in the poem is Carrickmacross, the nearest town to Inniskeen.

43 'Living in the Country': The poem recalls a time when Kavanagh was for the most part living in

Inniskeen. He was well looked after, even pampered by his sisters, Annie and Mary. He got bored with country living, especially in the evenings, and in order to escape from the sisters he would visit McNello's pub, a place he had never entered in his earlier years. He wasn't made especially welcome: the atmosphere was frosty and bitter. Kavanagh may have questioned his decision to leave Inniskeen but the reception he got locally meant he could never return to live there on a permanent basis.

46   'A Christmas Childhood': Kavanagh's father did indeed go outside the family house every Christmas morning and play Christmas music. Kavanagh wrote a number of Christmas poems, including 'Christmas Eve Remembered'.

51   'Love in a Meadow'. Toprass, mentioned in the penultimate line, is an Inniskeen place-name.

52   'Peace' is one of Kavanagh's classic country poems. His ambivalence about country versus city life is very evident. He captures the atmosphere with his distinctive simplicity. A saddle harrow removed the top of potato drills before the shoots broke the surface. It was shaped like a saddle and would not have been in general use throughout the country.

59   'Europe Is at War – Remembering Its Pastoral Peace' was first published in *The Irish Times* on 25 October 1939.

60   'Jim Larkin': There is a statue of Jim Larkin in O'Connell Street with a quotation from this poem. Kavanagh had little interest in politics, labour or trade unionism, but Larkin captured his imagination. According to his brother, 'Patrick was very proud and

satisfied with the finished poem, somewhat unusual for him. What's more, he bought a copy of the book, 1913: *Jim Larkin and the Dublin Lock-Out*, that was published by the Workers Union of Ireland in 1964 to commemorate the fiftieth anniversary of the event.'

62   'A Wreath for Tom Moore's Statue': Thomas Moore's statue stands on College Green, beside Trinity College and facing the Bank of Ireland. Moore (1779–1852) is best known for the songs he composed based on old Irish melodies, *Moore's Melodies*. A Thomas Moore Society was formed in Dublin in 1944 and this six-member group began the annual practice of laying a wreath on the poet's statue on 25 February. There was no public interest and about twenty spectators showed up. Patrick and Peter Kavanagh's Sunday-morning ritual saw them pass the statue on their way to lunch at Bernie's Café near O'Connell Street.

65   'On Raglan Road': Kavanagh met Hilda Moriarty on Raglan Road and fell for her. She was a strikingly beautiful medical student from west Kerry. She was many years younger than the poet and he knew that the daughter of Dr Paddy Moriarty of Dingle was never going to be his. They were not lovers; she was bemused by the eccentric older man and he was flattered to be in the company of such a beauty. He pursued her after a fashion but the sting of rejection quickly faded.

After Hilda married Limerick politician Donogh O'Malley, she and Kavanagh remained on good terms and she was concerned about his precarious lifestyle and ill-health. Her husband, far from being threatened, was fond of Kavanagh and was kind to him at Hilda's behest. Hilda and Kavanagh corresponded, although none of their letters survive. Kavanagh would periodically send telegrams to Dr

Hilda O'Malley in Limerick with a good tip for a horse. She was fond of a bet for the rest of her life.

The ballad became popular under the title 'On Raglan Road', sung to the traditional air 'The Dawning of the Day' ('Fáinne Geal an Lae'). Luke Kelly of the Dubliners made the song his own, giving it a strident, bittersweet edge. Kavanagh entrusted the song to Kelly the year before he died. Kelly recalled that this came about in the Bailey, where he met the poet. 'I got permission from the man himself,' said the singer. (Des Geraghty, *Luke Kelly: A Memoir*, Basement Press, 1994, p.39.) Kavanagh's brother Peter rejected this version of events: 'Never happened…total nonsense.' Kelly's story is credible, although maybe with a little embellishment on his part.

67　'The Great Hunger' was written while Kavanagh shared a bedsitter with his brother at 122 Morehampton Road in October 1941. It captures the loneliness, impoverishment and frustration of a small Monaghan farmer. It was innovative and courageous for its time and with it Kavanagh exploded the myth of the peasant poet.

70　'October 1943' was first published in the *Irish Press* on 27 October 1943.

73　'Kerr's Ass': Tommy Kerr, a house thatcher, lived up the road from the Kavanaghs. The big ass, as he was referred to, was borrowed by the Kavanaghs in poorer times. Eventually they would purchase their own horse and cart. This animal had a bit of a reputation locally for going slow to the market and running wild on the way home. This verse points to the self-sufficiency of small farmers and their dependence on each other for various tasks.

74　*Tarry Flynn*. London: Martin Brian & O'Keefe, 1972, pp. 102-3.

77　'Memory of My Father': Kavanagh and his father James were very close, even though their relationship was often contentious. The father was mindful that Patrick was the *elder* son and his successor on the farm. They discussed the issues of the day and more abstract subjects, the spiritual world and the afterlife.

In his final years James Kavanagh was stricken with Alzheimer's. His memory played tricks on him. Patrick tried to help him remember facts, faces and even music. It was a cruel blow to a man who took pride in reading the newspaper out loud to his family and customers, and writing letters for his illiterate neighbours.

80　Bridget Kavanagh died suddenly on 10 November 1945. She was seventy-three. This was a blow for the poet and his brother. Peter remembered: 'We felt bad about not being there with her when she died. There was some guilt on Patrick's part, you understand, that he had abandoned her and the farm and let her down.'

86　'If Ever You Go to Dublin Town': Kavanagh had a good singing voice and a good ear for a tune. There is a recording of him singing this song in *Almost Everything* (Claddagh Records, 1963.) He and Peter got a flat at 62 Pembroke Road in 1942. It was untidy and sparsely furnished but the location was convenient for the poet's ramblings in and out of the city, an easy walk to his haunts – pubs, shops, bookmakers, and bookshops – along Baggot Street.

92　'I Had a Future': Shortly after moving to Dublin in August 1939, Kavanagh lived in a bedsitter at 51

Upper Drumcondra Road. The poet is reflecting on the previous twelve years in Dublin, his modest living accommodation, his frustration and disillusionment. Peter came back from America in 1952 with $3000 in savings. The brothers decided to establish a forum for Patrick and *Kavanagh's Weekly* began its short run.

Kavanagh made himself known to the poet John Betjeman, who took up residence in Ireland in 1941 as press attaché to the British embassy. Betjeman introduced Kavanagh to John Lehmann, who published some of his work in *New Writing*, and to Cyril Connolly, who gave Kavanagh an outlet in *Horizon*. Betjeman frequented the Pearl Bar.

94   'The Rowley Mile' was first published in *The Bell* in January 1954. The stretch of pavement on which Kavanagh knew every crack and imperfection, from where he lived on Pembroke Road as far as Baggot Street Bridge, became the Rowley Mile, after the famous one-mile straight course in Newmarket, England. Peter Kavanagh said: 'Kavanagh began to back horses in 1949. He backed Nimbus, the winner of the Derby that year, on the strength of a tip he got from a friend outside Meservy's the Bookmakers. His walk along Merrion Row turned out to be a profitable one.'

The winner was bred by the legendary William Hill, a former Black-and-Tan, who had been stationed in Mallow, County Cork. Hill became the first multi-millionaire bookie and had horses in training on both sides of the Irish Sea. Nimbus, ridden by E.C. Elliot, came in at 7/1. Kavanagh had five shillings on the winner, which netted him a tidy return. He became a habitual, daily backer of horses, although he was chronically short of money.

96   Kavanagh was an admirer of Joyce. He, Brian O'Nolan, John Ryan, editor of *Envoy*, Anthony Cronin and Con Leventhal took part in the first Bloomsday pilgrimage on 16 June 1954. The day began at the Martello Tower in Sandycove, where the opening sequence of *Ulysses* is set. 'The cabby's shelter' was situated under the Loopline Bridge, west of the Custom House. The journey, after several stops for alcoholic refreshments, ended on a satisfying note in the back bar of the Bailey.

107   'The Hospital': Kavanagh was admitted to the Rialto Hospital, Dublin, on 31 March 1955 to have a cancerous lung removed. He had undergone tests and the family hoped it might be TB. Six months earlier he had gone to Baggot Street Hospital complaining of back pain near the shoulder but the doctor who examined him found no cause for concern. Bur Dr Keith Shaw, house surgeon at Rialto Hospital, confirmed that the tests indicated cancer. Surgery was the only option. Much would hinge on whether or not the visible (and unseen) cancer could be removed. Had Kavanagh presented himself sooner, the prognosis might have been better. He had been under the illusion that it was catarrh. The Rialto Hospital, then run by Dublin Corporation, was soon absorbed into St Kevin's (later St James's Hospital).

108ff.   'Canal Bank Walk' and 'Lines Written on a Seat on the Grand Canal, Dublin' were written after Kavanagh survived his operation for lung cancer and recuperated on the banks of the Grand Canal in the warm months of June and July 1955.

115   'Literary Adventures': John Lennon was an Inniskeen neighbour. John Jordan (1930-88) was a poet, short story writer and academic whom Kavanagh admired.

BIBLIOGRAPHY

BOOKS BY PATRICK KAVANAGH
(IN ORDER OF PUBLICATION)

Tarry Flynn. New York: Devin-Adair, 1949.

Self-Portrait. Dublin: Dolmen Press, 1964.

Collected Pruse. London: MacGibbon and Kee, 1967.

A Poet's Country: Selected Prose (ed. Antoinette Quinn). Dublin: Lilliput Press, 2003.

Collected Poems (ed. Antoinette Quinn). London: Allen Lane, 2004.

BOOKS BY OTHER AUTHORS

Browne, PJ. *Unfulfilled Promise: Memories of Donogh O'Malley*. Dublin: Currach Press, 2008.

Cronin, Anthony. *Dead as Doornails. Dublin*: Dolmen Press, 1976.

Geraghty, Des. *Luke Kelly: A Memoir*. Dublin: Basement Press, 1994.

McFadden, Hugh. *Selected Poems: John Jordan*. Dublin: Dedalus Press, 2008.

Quinn, Antoinette. *Patrick Kavanagh: A Biography*. Dublin: Gill and Macmillan, 2001.

NEWSPAPERS AND JOURNALS

Irish Press

Irish Independent

The Irish Times

National Observer

Weekly

New Statesman

Envoy

Poetry Ireland

Limerick Leader

INDEX OF TITLES

INDEX OF FIRST LINES